We hope this book has been informative and helpful on your journey to understanding and celebrating older adults. Thank you for your interest and support!

Title: Power Dynamics: Authoritarianism, Regimes, and Human Rights
Subtitle: Analyzing Authoritarian Regimes, Consolidation of Power, and Impact on Human Rights

Series: Global Perspectives: Exploring World Politics
By Jonathan A. Sinclair

Table of Contents

Introduction
Understanding Authoritarianism and its Significance

Authoritarianism is a form of government characterized by centralized control, limited political pluralism, and a lack of respect for civil liberties and human rights. In recent years, authoritarian regimes have gained increasing attention due to their consolidation of power, suppression of dissent, and the far-reaching consequences they have on human rights and civil liberties.

This chapter aims to provide a comprehensive understanding of authoritarianism, its underlying principles, and its significance in contemporary societies. By delving into the core characteristics and historical context of authoritarian regimes, we can gain valuable insights into the dynamics of power, governance, and the erosion of democratic principles.

To comprehend the nature of authoritarianism, we must first explore the fundamental features that define these regimes. Centralized control lies at the heart of authoritarian governance, with power concentrated in the hands of a single ruler or ruling elite. This concentration of power allows for swift decision-making but often at the expense of checks and balances, resulting in limited accountability and transparency.

Furthermore, understanding the historical context of authoritarian regimes is essential for comprehending their rise and persistence. Examining the emergence of authoritarianism in different regions, the factors that contribute to its sustenance, and the evolution of these regimes over time provides critical insights into their political, economic, and social dimensions.

The significance of studying authoritarianism extends beyond the political realm. Authoritarian regimes often curtail civil liberties, suppress dissent, and violate human rights, leading to a profound impact on individuals, communities, and society at large. By analyzing the consequences of authoritarian rule, we can shed light on the challenges faced by those living under such regimes and the broader implications for global stability and human rights advocacy.

In the following chapters, we will examine specific authoritarian regimes, such as China, Russia, Saudi Arabia, and North Korea, to gain a deeper understanding of their unique characteristics, historical context, consolidation of power, suppression of dissent, and the resulting impact on human rights and civil liberties.

By delving into these topics, we hope to foster a comprehensive understanding of authoritarianism, its implications for societies, and the urgent need to protect and promote human rights and democratic values.

Historical Context of Authoritarian Regimes

To fully comprehend the complexities of authoritarian regimes, it is essential to delve into their historical context. The rise and persistence of authoritarianism in various regions can be attributed to a range of historical, political, and socioeconomic factors. By examining the historical roots of these regimes, we can gain valuable insights into their evolution, modes of governance, and the underlying dynamics of power.

Throughout history, authoritarianism has manifested in different forms and contexts. From ancient empires and autocratic monarchies to modern-day totalitarian states, the roots of authoritarian regimes can be traced back to diverse historical periods and social conditions.

Understanding the historical context of authoritarian regimes requires an exploration of their emergence and consolidation. Historical events such as revolutions, wars, and economic crises often serve as catalysts for the rise of authoritarian leaders and movements. Additionally, the legacies of colonialism, post-colonial struggles, and the breakdown of democratic institutions have played a significant role in shaping the political landscape in many regions.

Furthermore, examining the historical context provides insights into the ideologies and belief systems that underpin authoritarian regimes. Some regimes draw inspiration from nationalist or ethnocentric ideologies, while others may exploit religious or ideological dogmas to justify their consolidation of power. Exploring these ideological foundations is crucial for understanding the rhetoric and propaganda employed by authoritarian leaders to manipulate public opinion and suppress dissent.

The historical context also sheds light on the strategies employed by authoritarian regimes to maintain their grip on power. Understanding the mechanisms of control, such as censorship, surveillance, and the manipulation of institutions, is key to comprehending the challenges faced by those advocating for human rights and civil liberties.

By analyzing the historical context of authoritarian regimes, we can gain a deeper understanding of their origins, their modes of governance, and the factors that contribute to their longevity. This knowledge is invaluable for comprehending the consolidation of power, the suppression of dissent, and the resulting impact on human rights and civil liberties.

In the following chapters, we will explore the historical contexts of specific authoritarian regimes, including China, Russia, Saudi Arabia, and North Korea. By examining their unique historical trajectories, we aim to uncover the underlying factors that have shaped these regimes and provide insights into their contemporary dynamics.

Through this exploration, we can gain a comprehensive understanding of the historical forces that have shaped authoritarianism, and the urgent need to challenge and address its implications for human rights and civil liberties.

Relationship Between Power, Human Rights, and Civil Liberties

At the heart of authoritarian regimes lies the intricate relationship between power, human rights, and civil liberties. Authoritarian leaders often consolidate and wield power in ways that directly impact the fundamental rights and freedoms of individuals and societies. Understanding this relationship is vital for comprehending the dynamics of governance, the erosion of rights, and the challenges faced by those seeking to promote human rights and civil liberties.

Power serves as the driving force behind authoritarian regimes, enabling leaders to exert control over institutions, society, and the lives of individuals. The concentration of power within a ruling elite or a single leader often leads to an imbalance of power relations and a lack of accountability. This concentration of power enables authoritarian leaders to suppress dissent, curtail civil liberties, and manipulate institutions to maintain their authority.

The consequences of unchecked power extend to the realm of human rights and civil liberties. Authoritarian regimes frequently infringe upon the rights and freedoms of their citizens, suppressing freedom of expression, assembly, and association. They may also curtail political participation, restrict access to information, and impose arbitrary arrests and detentions. The erosion of civil liberties under authoritarian rule has a profound impact on the lives of individuals and stifles the development of democratic values and institutions.

Examining the relationship between power and human rights reveals the vulnerability of individuals and communities living under authoritarian regimes. Power imbalances result in systemic human rights abuses, including torture, extrajudicial killings, forced disappearances, and widespread surveillance. The denial of human rights not only violates the inherent dignity of individuals but also undermines social cohesion, stability, and progress.

Civil liberties, which encompass the rights and freedoms granted to individuals by the state, are intrinsically linked to the exercise of power. Authoritarian regimes often curtail civil liberties to maintain control, restrict political opposition, and suppress dissenting voices. The erosion of civil liberties hampers social progress, limits individual agency, and obstructs the development of an open and inclusive society.

In the following chapters, we will examine specific authoritarian regimes, such as China, Russia, Saudi Arabia, and North Korea, to further explore the intricate relationship between power, human rights, and civil liberties. By analyzing the consolidation of power, the suppression of dissent, and the impact on human rights and civil liberties in these contexts, we can develop a comprehensive understanding of the challenges faced by individuals living under authoritarian rule.

Through this exploration, we aim to shed light on the urgent need to protect and promote human rights, challenge power imbalances, and advocate for the restoration of civil liberties in societies affected by authoritarianism.

Chapter 1: China

Evolution of China's Authoritarian Regime

China, with its rich history and vast population, has experienced significant transformations in its political landscape, leading to the emergence of an authoritarian regime. Understanding the evolution of China's authoritarianism is crucial for comprehending the dynamics of power, the role of the Communist Party, and the impact on human rights and civil liberties.

China's journey toward authoritarianism can be traced back to the establishment of the People's Republic of China in 1949. Under the leadership of Mao Zedong, the Communist Party of China (CPC) emerged as the dominant political force, implementing socialist policies and initiating widespread land reforms. The early years of the regime were characterized by the consolidation of power, rapid social transformation, and the suppression of dissent through campaigns such as the Great Leap Forward and the Cultural Revolution.

Following Mao's death in 1976, China entered a phase of political and economic transition under Deng Xiaoping. This marked the beginning of a more pragmatic approach to governance and economic development. The reform era brought about significant changes, including the adoption of market-oriented reforms, opening up to foreign investments, and the modernization of industries. However, despite these economic advancements, the CPC maintained tight political control and limited political pluralism.

Since the 1980s, China has experienced a paradoxical blend of economic liberalization and political repression. The Chinese government has promoted economic growth, transforming the country into a global economic powerhouse. However, this economic success has been accompanied by increasing restrictions on political dissent, censorship, and surveillance. The CPC remains the dominant political force, tightly controlling key institutions, media, and civil society organizations.

Under President Xi Jinping, who assumed power in 2012, China has witnessed a further consolidation of power and an intensified crackdown on dissent. Xi's leadership has been marked by efforts to strengthen the CPC's control over all aspects of society, including tightened internet controls, the suppression of human rights activists, and increased surveillance technologies.

The evolution of China's authoritarian regime has had profound implications for human rights and civil liberties. The government's suppression of dissent, restrictions on freedom of expression, and arbitrary detentions have raised concerns both domestically and internationally. The rapid economic development has improved living standards for many, but significant challenges remain in terms of labor rights, freedom of association, and protection of minority rights.

Understanding the evolution of China's authoritarian regime provides crucial insights into the consolidation of power, the role of the CPC, and the impact on human rights and civil liberties. In the subsequent sections of this chapter, we will delve deeper into the Communist Party's control, the economic transformation, and the specific concerns surrounding the suppression of dissent and human rights in China.

By examining the complexities of China's authoritarian regime, we can better comprehend the challenges faced by individuals and communities striving for greater rights and freedoms in this complex and influential nation.

Communist Party and State Control

The Communist Party of China (CPC) plays a central role in the governance of China, exercising significant control over the state apparatus, key institutions, and decision-making processes. Understanding the extent of CPC's authority and its impact on governance, human rights, and civil liberties is crucial for comprehending China's authoritarian regime.

The CPC's control can be traced back to the establishment of the People's Republic of China in 1949. Mao Zedong, the founding father of the People's Republic, led the CPC and established a one-party system that remains in place today. The party's supremacy is enshrined in the Chinese Constitution, which recognizes the CPC as the ruling party and grants it a leading role in all state affairs.

The CPC exercises control through various mechanisms. The party has a hierarchical structure, with the Central Committee at the apex and multiple levels of party organizations at the provincial, municipal, and local levels. Party members hold key positions in the government, military, judiciary, and state-owned enterprises, ensuring the CPC's influence permeates all spheres of society.

Key decision-making bodies within the party, such as the Politburo and the Standing Committee, hold significant power and influence over policy formulation and implementation. These bodies consist of high-ranking party officials, with the General Secretary serving as the top leader. The concentration of power in the hands of a few party leaders limits political pluralism and democratic processes.

The CPC's control extends beyond the party itself. The party exercises significant influence over the state apparatus, including the government, military, and judiciary. Party cells are established within these institutions, ensuring party oversight and loyalty. This integration of party and state blurs the line between party interests and the interests of the nation, enabling the CPC to maintain tight control over key decision-making processes.

State control of the media is another critical aspect of the CPC's authority. The party exercises strict censorship and imposes regulations on both traditional and digital media platforms. State-owned media outlets serve as mouthpieces for the party, disseminating official narratives and suppressing dissenting voices. The Great Firewall, a sophisticated system of internet censorship, further restricts access to information and curtails freedom of expression online.

The CPC's control has significant implications for human rights and civil liberties in China. The party's dominance limits political freedoms, stifles dissent, and restricts the development of independent civil society organizations. The CPC's influence over the state apparatus enables it to suppress human rights activism, curtail freedom of expression, and exert control over religious and ethnic minorities.

Understanding the Communist Party's control over the state apparatus provides critical insights into the functioning of China's authoritarian regime. In the subsequent sections of this chapter, we will further explore the economic transformation, the suppression of dissent, and the specific concerns surrounding human rights in China.

By examining the complexities of the Communist Party's control, we can gain a deeper understanding of the challenges faced by individuals and communities striving for greater rights and freedoms within the authoritarian framework of China.

Economic Transformation and Political Stability

China's economic transformation over the past few decades has been nothing short of remarkable. From a predominantly agrarian society to the world's second-largest economy, China's economic rise has had significant implications for its political stability and the dynamics of its authoritarian regime.

The economic reforms in China, initiated by Deng Xiaoping in the late 1970s, introduced market-oriented policies and opened up the country to foreign investments. This period of reform and opening up marked a departure from the centrally planned economy and ushered in an era of economic liberalization and rapid industrialization. As a result, China experienced exponential economic growth, lifted millions out of poverty, and became a global manufacturing hub.

The economic transformation has contributed to the stability of the authoritarian regime in several ways. First, by prioritizing economic development and improving living standards, the Communist Party of China (CPC) has gained legitimacy and support from the population. The party has maintained its hold on power by promising stability, economic prosperity, and improved standards of living for its citizens.

Second, the economic reforms have allowed the CPC to consolidate its authority through state-led capitalism. The party has maintained a significant presence in the economy through state-owned enterprises and strategic industries. This state control over key sectors of the economy enables the CPC to exert influence, regulate economic activities, and ensure its interests are aligned with national goals.

However, the economic transformation has not led to political liberalization or a transition to democracy. The CPC has maintained tight political control while allowing for limited economic freedoms. The party's control over key institutions, media, and civil society organizations ensures that economic development is pursued within the boundaries set by the party's agenda.

The relationship between economic growth and political stability in China is complex. On one hand, economic growth has contributed to the regime's stability by providing employment opportunities, reducing social inequalities, and improving living standards. On the other hand, rapid economic development has also led to social tensions, income disparities, and environmental challenges, which the regime has had to manage to maintain stability.

The CPC has employed various strategies to address these challenges, including targeted poverty alleviation programs, urbanization policies, and environmental regulations. The party's ability to navigate these economic and social challenges while maintaining political control has been a key factor in its continued stability.

Understanding the interplay between economic transformation and political stability provides valuable insights into the dynamics of China's authoritarian regime. In the subsequent sections of this chapter, we will further explore the suppression of dissent, human rights concerns, and the impact of economic development on civil liberties in China.

By examining the complexities of China's economic transformation and its implications for political stability, we can gain a deeper understanding of the challenges faced by individuals and communities striving for greater rights and freedoms within the authoritarian framework of China.

Suppression of Dissent and Human Rights Concerns

China's authoritarian regime is known for its tight control over dissenting voices and the suppression of political opposition. Understanding the methods employed by the Communist Party of China (CPC) to silence dissent and the human rights concerns that arise from such practices is crucial for comprehending the dynamics of China's authoritarian rule.

The suppression of dissent in China takes various forms. One key mechanism is strict control over freedom of expression. The CPC maintains a pervasive system of censorship and employs sophisticated technologies to monitor and restrict online content. The Great Firewall, a comprehensive internet censorship system, blocks access to foreign websites and social media platforms, limiting the flow of information and stifling freedom of expression. Dissenting opinions, criticism of the government, and discussions on sensitive topics are heavily censored and can lead to severe consequences for those who dare to challenge the party line.

The Chinese government also employs legal and judicial tools to suppress dissent. Laws related to national security, subversion, and state secrets are broadly defined and often used to target activists, human rights defenders, and dissidents. These individuals face arbitrary arrests, enforced disappearances, and unfair trials, with little regard for due process or the rule of law. The use of extralegal measures, such as enforced residential surveillance and secret detentions, further erodes the rights and freedoms of individuals who dare to voice their opposition.

Another area of concern is the restriction of civil society and independent organizations. The CPC tightly controls non-governmental organizations (NGOs), trade unions, and religious groups, requiring them to register with the government and operate within strict boundaries. Organizations that engage in activities perceived as threatening to the party's rule or promoting values inconsistent with the government's ideology face harassment, closure, or imprisonment of their members.

These suppression tactics have significant human rights implications. Freedom of expression, association, and peaceful assembly are severely curtailed in China. Human rights defenders, activists, journalists, and lawyers who strive for social justice and advocate for human rights face harassment, intimidation, and imprisonment. Vulnerable groups, such as ethnic and religious minorities, also experience discrimination, restrictions on cultural expression, and surveillance.

International scrutiny and human rights advocacy have brought some of these concerns to the forefront. Human rights organizations, journalists, and foreign governments have highlighted cases of arbitrary detention, torture, and forced labor in China. The treatment of Uighur Muslims in Xinjiang and the crackdown on pro-democracy activists in Hong Kong have raised international concern and condemnation.

Understanding the suppression of dissent and human rights concerns in China provides crucial insights into the challenges faced by individuals striving for greater rights and freedoms within the authoritarian framework. In the subsequent sections of this chapter, we will delve deeper into the specific human rights violations, international responses, and the impact of the suppression of dissent on civil liberties in China.

By examining the complexities of the CPC's suppression tactics and the resulting human rights concerns, we can gain a deeper understanding of the struggles faced by individuals and communities striving for greater rights and freedoms within China's authoritarian regime.

Chapter 2: Russia
Post-Soviet Political Landscape

The collapse of the Soviet Union in 1991 marked a pivotal moment in Russian history and brought about significant changes in the country's political landscape. Understanding the transformation of Russia's political system in the post-Soviet era is crucial for comprehending the dynamics of its authoritarian regime under the leadership of Vladimir Putin.

Following the dissolution of the Soviet Union, Russia embarked on a path of political and economic transition. The initial years were characterized by political instability, economic turmoil, and social upheaval. Yeltsin's presidency, marked by economic reforms, privatization, and political turbulence, laid the foundation for the emerging political landscape in post-Soviet Russia.

The 1993 constitutional crisis, during which Yeltsin dissolved the Russian parliament and faced armed opposition, highlighted the fragility of democratic institutions in the country. The adoption of a new constitution in 1993 centralized power in the presidency and established a strong executive branch. This concentration of power paved the way for the consolidation of authority under Vladimir Putin.

Vladimir Putin's rise to power in 1999 marked a significant turning point in Russian politics. Putin, a former KGB officer, presented himself as a stabilizing force and sought to restore Russia's global standing. He implemented measures to centralize power, weaken political opposition, and increase state control over key institutions.

One of Putin's early actions was the suppression of independent media and the consolidation of state control over television networks. Critical media outlets faced pressure, censorship, and state takeovers, limiting the availability of unbiased information and silencing dissenting voices. The state's influence over the media landscape played a crucial role in shaping public opinion and maintaining support for Putin's regime.

The political system under Putin has been characterized by a tightly controlled electoral process. Opposition parties face significant obstacles, including restricted access to media, limitations on campaign activities, and allegations of electoral fraud. The dominance of the ruling United Russia party and the lack of genuine political competition have led to a limited pluralism and weakened checks and balances.

Another notable aspect of the post-Soviet political landscape in Russia is the relationship between the state and business elites. The Putin regime has been associated with a high degree of state intervention in the economy, particularly through the control of strategic industries and state-owned enterprises. The close ties between political and economic elites have reinforced the consolidation of power and limited the emergence of independent power centers.

Understanding the transformation of Russia's political landscape in the post-Soviet era provides valuable insights into the functioning of its authoritarian regime. In the subsequent sections of this chapter, we will delve deeper into the consolidation of power under Vladimir Putin, state control of media and opposition, and the implications for human rights and democratic institutions in Russia.

By examining the complexities of the post-Soviet political landscape, we can gain a deeper understanding of the challenges faced by individuals and communities striving for greater rights and freedoms within the authoritarian framework of Russia.

Consolidation of Power under Vladimir Putin

Vladimir Putin's rise to power in 1999 marked a significant turning point in Russian politics. Understanding the consolidation of power under Putin is crucial for comprehending the dynamics of Russia's authoritarian regime and its implications for human rights and democratic institutions.

Putin's early years in office were characterized by efforts to centralize power and weaken political opposition. Through a series of strategic moves, he sought to establish control over key institutions and reshape the political landscape to his advantage. One of the key instruments used by Putin to consolidate power was the manipulation of the political system.

Putin's regime systematically weakened political opposition parties and independent voices. Opposition leaders faced various obstacles, including legal challenges, harassment, and restrictions on their activities. The state-controlled media played a significant role in shaping public opinion and ensuring a favorable narrative for Putin and his regime. Critical voices were marginalized, and dissenting opinions were suppressed.

In 2004, Putin implemented a series of constitutional changes that further consolidated his authority. These changes included the abolition of direct elections for regional governors and the establishment of a system where governors are appointed by the president. This move reduced the autonomy of regional leaders and strengthened the centralization of power in the presidency.

Another critical aspect of Putin's consolidation of power was the control over the security apparatus. Putin's background as a former KGB officer enabled him to exert influence over the security services, ensuring their loyalty to the regime. This control over the security apparatus helped suppress dissent and maintain political stability.

Putin's regime also implemented measures to weaken civil society organizations and independent institutions. Non-governmental organizations (NGOs) faced increased scrutiny and restrictions, particularly those receiving foreign funding. Laws were passed to limit the activities of NGOs, branding them as "foreign agents" and subjecting them to intrusive regulations and inspections.

The consolidation of power under Putin was not limited to the political realm. The regime extended its influence over strategic sectors of the economy, often through state-owned enterprises or close ties to oligarchs. This intertwining of political and economic power reinforced the regime's control and limited the emergence of independent power centers.

The consolidation of power under Putin has had significant implications for human rights and democratic institutions in Russia. The lack of genuine political competition, restrictions on freedom of expression, and the suppression of dissent have resulted in limited pluralism and weakened checks and balances. The regime's control over key institutions and the close nexus between political and economic elites have hindered the development of a transparent and accountable governance system.

Understanding the consolidation of power under Vladimir Putin provides valuable insights into the functioning of Russia's authoritarian regime. In the subsequent sections of this chapter, we will explore the state control of media and opposition, the implications for human rights, and the challenges faced by civil society in Russia.

By examining the complexities of the consolidation of power, we can gain a deeper understanding of the challenges faced by individuals and communities striving for greater rights and freedoms within the authoritarian framework of Russia.

State Control of Media and Opposition

The control of media and opposition is a crucial element in understanding the dynamics of Russia's authoritarian regime under Vladimir Putin. This chapter explores the state's extensive control over media outlets and its implications for the functioning of a free and independent press, as well as the suppression of political opposition.

Under Putin's leadership, the Russian government has implemented various measures to ensure control over the media landscape. The state has gained significant influence over both traditional and digital media platforms, limiting the availability of diverse and independent sources of information. Key methods employed by the regime include ownership and funding control, restrictive legislation, and targeted harassment of journalists.

One of the strategies used by the Russian government is the direct or indirect ownership of major media outlets. State-controlled companies or individuals with close ties to the government acquire ownership stakes in influential media organizations, thereby exerting influence over editorial policies and content. This control allows the government to shape the narrative and ensure a favorable portrayal of the regime.

In addition to ownership control, the Russian government has employed restrictive legislation to suppress dissent and limit freedom of the press. Laws have been introduced that criminalize defamation, restrict the activities of NGOs, and impose strict regulations on online platforms. These laws are often applied selectively to target critical voices, independent journalists, and opposition figures, leading to self-censorship and the silencing of dissent.

The regime's control over the media is not limited to legal measures. Harassment and intimidation of journalists critical of the government have become common. Journalists face threats, physical attacks, and imprisonment for their work. The high-profile cases of journalists like Anna Politkovskaya and Boris Nemtsov highlight the risks faced by those who challenge the government's narrative.

The Russian government also employs sophisticated methods of information control and manipulation. State-sponsored propaganda, disinformation campaigns, and online trolls are used to shape public opinion and discredit opposition voices. The state-controlled media actively promotes the government's agenda, while dissenting voices are marginalized or labeled as unpatriotic.

The control of media is closely intertwined with the suppression of political opposition in Russia. Opposition parties face significant obstacles, including limited access to media platforms, restrictions on campaign activities, and allegations of electoral fraud. The dominance of the ruling United Russia party and the lack of genuine political competition undermine democratic processes and impede the development of a pluralistic political system.

The state's control of media and opposition has significant implications for human rights and democratic institutions in Russia. The absence of a free and independent press limits the availability of unbiased information and critical scrutiny of the government's actions. It also hinders the ability of citizens to make informed decisions and engage in meaningful political discourse.

Understanding the state control of media and opposition provides valuable insights into the challenges faced by individuals and communities striving for greater rights and freedoms within the authoritarian framework of Russia. In the subsequent sections of this chapter, we will explore the implications of state control over media and opposition for human rights, democratic institutions, and civil liberties in Russia.

By examining the complexities of state control over media and opposition, we can gain a deeper understanding of the challenges faced by individuals and communities striving for greater rights and freedoms within the authoritarian framework of Russia.

Implications for Human Rights and Democratic Institutions

The authoritarian regime under Vladimir Putin in Russia has had significant implications for human rights and democratic institutions in the country. This chapter examines the consequences of the regime's policies and practices on the protection of human rights, the functioning of democratic institutions, and the overall state of civil liberties in Russia.

One of the most concerning aspects of Putin's regime is the shrinking space for civil liberties and fundamental human rights. Freedom of expression and freedom of the press are curtailed through state control of media and restrictions on dissenting voices. Journalists, activists, and political opponents face harassment, intimidation, and even violence for their work or their criticism of the government.

The regime's control over media outlets limits access to unbiased information, hindering the public's ability to make informed decisions and engage in meaningful political discourse. The absence of a free and independent press undermines transparency, accountability, and the ability of citizens to hold those in power to account.

The rule of law and judicial independence have also been undermined under Putin's regime. The politicization of the judiciary and the influence of the executive branch in judicial appointments have eroded the impartiality and integrity of the legal system. This has resulted in a lack of effective remedies for human rights violations and a climate of impunity for those responsible.

The regime's efforts to suppress political opposition have weakened democratic institutions and limited political pluralism. Opposition parties face obstacles in participating in elections, with allegations of electoral fraud and limited access to media platforms. The dominance of the ruling United Russia party and the lack of genuine political competition undermine the principles of a vibrant and inclusive democracy.

Human rights abuses, including arbitrary detentions, torture, and restrictions on freedom of assembly, are prevalent in Russia. The government has targeted specific groups, including LGBTQ+ individuals, ethnic minorities, and human rights defenders. Discrimination, persecution, and violence against these marginalized communities have intensified under the authoritarian regime.

The implications of the regime's policies and practices extend beyond Russia's borders. The suppression of civil society and the manipulation of information have an impact on regional and global dynamics. The government's influence on neighboring countries, the weaponization of energy resources, and attempts to undermine democratic processes in other nations raise concerns about the regime's efforts to project power and exert influence beyond its borders.

The situation in Russia highlights the challenges faced by human rights defenders, civil society organizations, and individuals striving for greater rights and freedoms. International cooperation and advocacy play a crucial role in addressing the human rights violations and protecting democratic institutions.

Understanding the implications for human rights and democratic institutions under Putin's regime provides valuable insights into the challenges faced by individuals and communities striving for greater rights and freedoms within the authoritarian framework of Russia. In the subsequent sections of this chapter, we will explore the role of international organizations, activism, and the potential for change in promoting human rights and democratic values.

By examining the complexities of the implications for human rights and democratic institutions, we can gain a deeper understanding of the challenges faced by individuals and communities striving for greater rights and freedoms within the authoritarian framework of Russia.

Chapter 3: Saudi Arabia
Saudi Monarchy and Political System

Understanding the Saudi monarchy and its political system is essential for analyzing the dynamics of authoritarianism and its impact on human rights and civil liberties in Saudi Arabia. This chapter explores the structure of the monarchy, its role in governance, and the implications for political participation and power distribution in the country.

Saudi Arabia is an absolute monarchy, meaning power is concentrated in the hands of the ruling Al Saud family. The monarchy traces its roots back to the establishment of the modern Saudi state in 1932 by King Abdulaziz Al Saud. The Saudi royal family holds significant control over key institutions, resources, and decision-making processes.

The king, as the head of state and government, wields ultimate executive authority in Saudi Arabia. The position of king is hereditary, with the throne passing from one generation to the next within the Al Saud family. The king exercises broad powers, including the appointment of top government officials, the formulation of policies, and the interpretation of Sharia law.

Under the monarchy, there is a dual legal system in place. The formal legal system is based on statutes and regulations, while Islamic law, or Sharia, is considered a primary source of legislation. The interpretation and application of Sharia law are entrusted to religious scholars and judges, who play a significant role in the legal system.

The Saudi political system is characterized by limited political participation and a lack of meaningful representation. There are no political parties, and public elections are limited to municipal councils with restricted powers. The government has implemented top-down reforms aimed at centralizing decision-making processes and maintaining stability, rather than promoting democratic governance.

The Consultative Assembly, or Majlis al-Shura, serves as an advisory body to the king. Its members are appointed by the king rather than elected by the public. While the assembly has been given a more prominent role in recent years, its powers remain limited, and it lacks the authority to legislate or hold the government accountable.

The Saudi monarchy's tight grip on power has been reinforced by a system of patronage and alliances with various factions within the country. The royal family maintains a complex network of alliances with religious leaders, tribal elites, and business magnates, ensuring loyalty and support for the regime. This network allows the monarchy to maintain control and suppress dissent.

The political system in Saudi Arabia has significant implications for human rights and civil liberties. Freedom of expression, assembly, and association are severely restricted, and criticism of the government or the royal family can result in harsh penalties. Women's rights have been a particular area of concern, although recent reforms have brought some improvements, such as allowing women to drive and expanding their economic participation.

Understanding the Saudi monarchy and political system provides valuable insights into the challenges faced by individuals and communities striving for greater rights and freedoms within the authoritarian framework of Saudi Arabia. In the subsequent sections of this chapter, we will explore the role of religion and Sharia law, the suppression of dissent, and the impact on human rights and civil liberties.

By examining the complexities of the Saudi monarchy and political system, we can gain a deeper understanding of the challenges faced by individuals and communities striving for greater rights and freedoms within the authoritarian framework of Saudi Arabia.

Role of Religion and Sharia Law

The role of religion and Sharia law is central to understanding the dynamics of authoritarianism and its impact on human rights and civil liberties in Saudi Arabia. This chapter explores the influence of religion, the implementation of Sharia law, and its implications for governance, social norms, and individual freedoms in the country.

Saudi Arabia follows a strict interpretation of Sunni Islam known as Wahhabism or Salafism. The alliance between the Saudi royal family and the religious establishment has played a crucial role in consolidating the monarchy's power and shaping the country's social and legal framework.

Sharia law serves as a primary source of legislation in Saudi Arabia. It is a comprehensive legal system based on Islamic principles derived from the Quran and the teachings of the Prophet Muhammad. The interpretation and application of Sharia law are overseen by religious scholars and judges who form part of the country's judicial system.

The influence of Sharia law permeates various aspects of Saudi society, including personal status laws, criminal justice, and public behavior. Family matters, such as marriage, divorce, and inheritance, are governed by Sharia law, often leading to gender-based disparities and restrictions on the rights of women. The enforcement of strict gender segregation, dress codes, and moral policing are also rooted in interpretations of Sharia law.

The religious police, known as the Committee for the Promotion of Virtue and the Prevention of Vice, have a prominent role in enforcing religious norms and moral codes in public spaces. Their authority extends to monitoring and regulating behavior, including the prohibition of activities deemed contrary to Islamic teachings.

The role of religion and Sharia law in Saudi Arabia has significant implications for human rights and civil liberties. Freedom of religion is limited, with the practice of religions other than Islam restricted. Criticism of Islam or religious figures can lead to severe consequences, including legal prosecution. Non-Muslim religious practices are largely prohibited, and places of worship for non-Muslims are rare.

The strict interpretation of Islamic law and the influence of religious authorities contribute to restrictions on freedom of expression, particularly when it comes to challenging religious doctrine or expressing dissenting views. Journalists, activists, and intellectuals face censorship, harassment, and imprisonment for expressing opinions deemed contrary to the religious or political establishment.

Understanding the role of religion and Sharia law provides valuable insights into the challenges faced by individuals and communities striving for greater rights and freedoms within the authoritarian framework of Saudi Arabia. In the subsequent sections of this chapter, we will explore the suppression of dissent, women's rights, and the impact on human rights and civil liberties.

By examining the complexities of the role of religion and Sharia law, we can gain a deeper understanding of the challenges faced by individuals and communities striving for greater rights and freedoms within the authoritarian framework of Saudi Arabia.

Suppression of Dissent and Women's Rights

The suppression of dissent and restrictions on women's rights are prominent features of the authoritarian regime in Saudi Arabia. This chapter delves into the mechanisms of dissent suppression, the challenges faced by activists and critics, and the specific issues surrounding women's rights in the country.

The Saudi regime maintains a tight grip on dissent through a combination of legal measures, surveillance, and intimidation tactics. Criticism of the government or the royal family is met with severe consequences, including arbitrary detention, imprisonment, and sometimes even extrajudicial measures. The government has targeted journalists, bloggers, human rights activists, and intellectuals who speak out against the regime's policies or advocate for democratic reforms.

Freedom of expression is heavily curtailed in Saudi Arabia. The government exercises strict control over the media, which is predominantly state-owned or influenced by the ruling family. Journalists and media professionals face censorship, self-censorship, and harassment, leading to a climate of fear and limited public debate on sensitive topics.

In recent years, the Saudi regime has initiated a crackdown on dissent, resulting in the arrest and detention of prominent activists and intellectuals. The arbitrary nature of these arrests, lack of due process, and reports of torture and ill-treatment in detention centers have raised serious concerns about human rights violations in the country.

Women's rights in Saudi Arabia have been a subject of international scrutiny. The country has implemented some reforms in recent years to improve gender equality, such as allowing women to drive and expanding their access to education and employment. However, systemic discrimination and a patriarchal societal framework still limit women's rights and freedoms.

The guardianship system, which requires women to obtain permission from a male guardian for various activities, remains a significant barrier to women's autonomy. Women face restrictions on travel, marriage, divorce, and access to healthcare without the consent of a male guardian. Although reforms have been introduced to mitigate some aspects of the guardianship system, fundamental changes are still needed to ensure gender equality and women's full participation in society.

Activists advocating for women's rights and gender equality face significant risks in Saudi Arabia. Women who challenge the status quo and speak out for their rights can face arrests, intimidation, and social ostracism. While some progress has been made, it is essential to continue addressing the systemic obstacles and cultural norms that perpetuate gender inequality in the country.

Understanding the suppression of dissent and the challenges surrounding women's rights provides valuable insights into the struggles faced by individuals and communities striving for greater rights and freedoms within the authoritarian framework of Saudi Arabia. In the subsequent sections of this chapter, we will explore the regional influence of Saudi Arabia, women's activism, and the impact on human rights and civil liberties.

By examining the complexities of the suppression of dissent and women's rights, we can gain a deeper understanding of the challenges faced by individuals and communities striving for greater rights and freedoms within the authoritarian framework of Saudi Arabia.

Saudi Arabia's Influence in the Middle East

Saudi Arabia wields significant influence in the Middle East, both politically and religiously. This chapter explores the various dimensions of Saudi Arabia's regional influence, including its role in regional conflicts, promotion of Wahhabism, and geopolitical dynamics in the Middle East.

Saudi Arabia's regional influence is largely shaped by its oil wealth and the custodianship of Islam's two holiest sites, Mecca and Medina. The country's vast oil reserves and its role as a major exporter of oil give it substantial economic leverage and allow it to shape energy policies in the region. The economic influence extends to foreign aid and investments, which Saudi Arabia utilizes as a tool for promoting its interests and building alliances with other countries in the Middle East.

Religiously, Saudi Arabia promotes and exports the strict interpretation of Sunni Islam known as Wahhabism or Salafism. Through financial support, educational institutions, and the dissemination of religious materials, Saudi Arabia has spread its influence and established itself as a significant player in shaping the religious landscape of the Middle East. The export of Wahhabism has been criticized for contributing to the rise of extremism and intolerance in some areas.

Saudi Arabia's regional influence is particularly pronounced in the context of regional conflicts. The country has played a key role in supporting various factions in conflicts such as the Syrian civil war, the Yemeni crisis, and the regional struggle against Iran. Through financial assistance, arms supplies, and diplomatic engagement, Saudi Arabia seeks to influence the outcomes of these conflicts and advance its geopolitical interests.

However, Saudi Arabia's regional influence is not without challenges and complexities. Its rivalry with Iran for regional dominance has fueled proxy conflicts and sectarian tensions across the Middle East. The ongoing conflict in Yemen, where Saudi Arabia leads a military coalition against Houthi rebels supported by Iran, highlights the complexities and humanitarian consequences of Saudi Arabia's regional involvement.

Saudi Arabia's influence in the Middle East intersects with its domestic policies and the suppression of dissent. The government often uses its regional stature to stifle criticism and garner support from regional allies. The human rights situation in Saudi Arabia has drawn international criticism, particularly in relation to its regional influence and involvement in conflicts.

Understanding Saudi Arabia's regional influence is crucial to comprehending the power dynamics and geopolitical complexities of the Middle East. In the subsequent sections of this chapter, we will explore the human rights implications, the role of international actors, and the broader impact of Saudi Arabia's regional influence on human rights and civil liberties.

By examining Saudi Arabia's influence in the Middle East, we can gain insights into the interplay between regional politics, religious dynamics, and authoritarian practices, shedding light on the broader consequences for human rights and civil liberties in the region.

Chapter 4: North Korea
Kim Dynasty and Totalitarian Rule

The Kim dynasty and totalitarian rule have been defining features of North Korea's political landscape for decades. This chapter explores the rise of the Kim dynasty, the consolidation of power, and the mechanisms of totalitarian control in North Korea.

The Kim dynasty began with the country's founder, Kim Il-sung, who established the Democratic People's Republic of Korea (DPRK) in 1948. Kim Il-sung cultivated a personality cult around himself, presenting himself as the nation's revered leader and implementing policies of Juche, a doctrine emphasizing self-reliance and the glorification of the state. Under his rule, North Korea adopted a system of one-man rule, concentrating power in the hands of the supreme leader.

After Kim Il-sung's death in 1994, his son Kim Jong-il assumed power, continuing the lineage of the Kim dynasty. Kim Jong-il further strengthened the personality cult and solidified the totalitarian control over all aspects of North Korean society. The state-controlled media portrayed him as an infallible leader, while dissent and opposition were ruthlessly suppressed.

Following Kim Jong-il's death in 2011, his son, Kim Jong-un, took over as the leader of North Korea, perpetuating the Kim dynasty's rule. Under Kim Jong-un, the personality cult has reached unprecedented levels, with the leader being hailed as the "Supreme Leader" and the "Great Successor." The regime has continued to prioritize the military, nuclear ambitions, and the pursuit of self-reliance, despite the immense human and economic costs.

Totalitarian control in North Korea extends to all aspects of life, encompassing politics, the economy, and social and cultural spheres. The state exercises strict surveillance and propaganda machinery, maintaining a monopoly over information and indoctrinating the population from an early age. The regime enforces strict loyalty to the leadership, punishing any signs of dissent or criticism, which can lead to imprisonment, forced labor, and even execution.

The totalitarian control is exemplified by the songbun system, which categorizes individuals into different social classes based on their loyalty to the regime. This system determines access to education, employment, and social benefits, perpetuating social inequalities and discrimination.

The pervasive control extends to the economy, where the state maintains a command economy, tightly regulating all economic activities and limiting individual freedoms. The majority of resources are allocated to the military and the ruling elite, while the general population faces economic hardships, food shortages, and limited access to basic necessities.

Understanding the Kim dynasty and the mechanisms of totalitarian rule provides valuable insights into the extreme power dynamics, the suppression of dissent, and the dire human rights situation in North Korea. In the subsequent sections of this chapter, we will delve into state propaganda, human rights abuses, international responses, and the regional security concerns arising from North Korea's totalitarian rule.

By examining the Kim dynasty and totalitarian rule, we can gain a deeper understanding of the complexities and challenges faced by the people of North Korea and the impact of such authoritarian practices on human rights and civil liberties.

State Propaganda and Isolationism

State propaganda and isolationism are integral components of North Korea's governance, shaping its political, social, and cultural landscape. This chapter examines the extensive use of propaganda and the policy of isolationism employed by the North Korean regime to maintain control over its population and project a specific image to the outside world.

State propaganda plays a fundamental role in North Korea, serving as a powerful tool for regime consolidation and indoctrination. The regime exercises strict control over the media, effectively monopolizing information and manipulating public opinion. State-controlled newspapers, television, and radio broadcast a constant stream of propaganda, exalting the leadership, promoting loyalty to the state, and perpetuating the cult of personality surrounding the ruling Kim dynasty.

Portraits, statues, and murals of the leaders are ubiquitous throughout the country, reinforcing their omnipresence and invoking a sense of awe and reverence. Schools and workplaces regularly hold political education sessions, where individuals are subjected to ideological indoctrination and required to express unwavering loyalty to the regime. North Korean citizens are expected to demonstrate absolute devotion to the leaders and to internalize the regime's ideology from an early age.

The regime also employs a policy of isolationism, isolating the country from external influences and controlling the flow of information. North Korea strictly regulates foreign media, blocking access to the internet and external television broadcasts. The government operates a closed intranet system, known as Kwangmyong, which provides limited access to state-approved information. This isolationist policy aims to prevent the infiltration of outside ideas and narratives that could challenge the regime's control.

Isolationism extends beyond the control of information to strict restrictions on travel and interaction with the outside world. North Korean citizens face severe limitations on international travel, with most individuals being prohibited from leaving the country. In addition, foreigners are heavily monitored during their stay in North Korea, with access to certain areas and interactions with locals closely monitored and controlled.

The regime's use of state propaganda and isolationism creates a tightly controlled information environment and perpetuates a sense of nationalistic fervor and loyalty to the regime. However, it also reinforces the isolation and ignorance of the population, limiting their exposure to alternative perspectives, ideas, and information from the outside world.

The impact of state propaganda and isolationism extends beyond North Korea's borders. The regime's efforts to project a specific image and control information flow pose challenges to understanding the realities within the country and engaging in meaningful dialogue. The international community's ability to assess the human rights situation and address the challenges posed by the North Korean regime is hindered by the regime's deliberate isolationist policies.

By examining the state propaganda machinery and isolationist policies in North Korea, we can gain insights into the mechanisms of control, the manipulation of information, and the challenges faced by the North Korean population. In the subsequent sections of this chapter, we will delve into human rights abuses, international responses, and the regional security concerns arising from North Korea's state propaganda and isolationist practices.

Understanding state propaganda and isolationism is essential for comprehending the power dynamics, information control, and the limitations on human rights and civil liberties within North Korea.

Human Rights Abuses and International Response

North Korea has been widely criticized for its severe and systematic human rights abuses, which have drawn international attention and concern. This chapter examines the nature of human rights abuses in North Korea and the responses of the international community to address these violations.

Human rights abuses in North Korea encompass a wide range of violations, including political repression, arbitrary detentions, forced labor, torture, and extrajudicial killings. The regime's totalitarian control allows little room for dissent, and any perceived opposition or criticism of the leadership is met with harsh punishment. The prison camp system, including political prison camps such as Camp 14 and Camp 22, has been a subject of significant international concern. Reports indicate that these camps house thousands of political prisoners subjected to forced labor, torture, and inhumane conditions.

The rights to freedom of expression, association, and assembly are severely curtailed in North Korea. The state exercises strict control over media outlets, allowing only state-sanctioned information to be disseminated. Internet access is limited and closely monitored, preventing free access to information and suppressing freedom of expression. Any form of organized dissent or independent political activity is swiftly suppressed.

The international community has responded to these human rights abuses through various mechanisms. The United Nations has played a central role in documenting and condemning human rights violations in North Korea. The UN Human Rights Council has established a Commission of Inquiry (COI) to investigate these abuses and has produced several reports detailing the gravity of the situation. These reports have shed light on the scale and severity of human rights violations and called for accountability.

Efforts to address human rights abuses in North Korea have also involved non-governmental organizations (NGOs) and civil society groups. These organizations work to raise awareness, provide support to North Korean defectors, and advocate for human rights at the international level. They play a crucial role in documenting abuses, collecting testimonies, and giving a voice to the victims of human rights violations.

International sanctions have been another response to human rights abuses in North Korea. These sanctions aim to pressure the regime to improve its human rights record by imposing restrictions on trade, finance, and diplomatic relations. While the effectiveness of sanctions in achieving concrete improvements remains a subject of debate, they serve as a symbolic measure to signal international disapproval.

However, engaging with North Korea on human rights issues has proven challenging due to the regime's resistance and its preference for isolation. The North Korean government has often denied allegations of human rights abuses and characterized international scrutiny as interference in its internal affairs. Nonetheless, the international community continues to emphasize the importance of addressing human rights concerns alongside other diplomatic efforts.

By examining the human rights abuses in North Korea and the responses of the international community, we can gain a deeper understanding of the challenges faced in promoting human rights and addressing the dire situation within the country. In the subsequent sections of this chapter, we will explore the role of international organizations, advocacy for human rights, and the complex dynamics of engaging with North Korea on human rights issues.

Understanding the human rights abuses and the international response is crucial in addressing the power dynamics, suppression of dissent, and the imperative to protect human rights and civil liberties in North Korea.

Nuclear Ambitions and Regional Security Concerns

North Korea's nuclear ambitions and its pursuit of weapons of mass destruction have raised significant regional and international security concerns. This chapter examines the evolution of North Korea's nuclear program, its implications for regional stability, and the responses of the international community to address the nuclear threat.

North Korea's nuclear program dates back to the 1960s and has been a subject of increasing concern since the early 1990s. The regime's pursuit of nuclear weapons is driven by multiple factors, including regime survival, national security considerations, and leverage in international negotiations. The development of nuclear capabilities is seen as a deterrent against perceived external threats and a means to assert the regime's influence on the global stage.

North Korea conducted its first nuclear test in 2006, followed by subsequent tests in 2009, 2013, 2016, and 2017, indicating steady progress in its nuclear capabilities. These tests have raised alarm bells among neighboring countries and the international community, heightening concerns about the potential use of nuclear weapons and the destabilizing impact on regional security.

The possession of nuclear weapons by North Korea has several regional security implications. Firstly, it threatens the stability of the Korean Peninsula, raising the risk of a nuclear conflict that could have catastrophic consequences. The potential for miscalculation, escalation, and unintended consequences is a constant worry.

Secondly, North Korea's nuclear program has sparked a regional arms race, as neighboring countries seek to bolster their own defenses in response to the perceived threat. This further complicates the security landscape and increases the potential for a volatile and dangerous environment in Northeast Asia.

Furthermore, the nuclear ambitions of North Korea have strained relations with major powers such as the United States, China, Russia, and Japan. The international community has responded to North Korea's nuclear provocations with a series of sanctions, diplomatic efforts, and negotiations aimed at denuclearization and regional stability. However, finding a sustainable solution to the North Korean nuclear issue has proven to be a complex and challenging task.

Efforts to address the nuclear threat from North Korea have involved multilateral diplomatic initiatives, such as the Six-Party Talks involving China, Japan, Russia, South

Korea, the United States, and North Korea. These talks, aimed at achieving denuclearization, have faced numerous setbacks and have not yielded significant progress in recent years.

The international community has also imposed economic sanctions on North Korea, aiming to curtail its access to resources, technology, and financing that could be used to advance its nuclear program. However, the effectiveness of these sanctions is limited by North Korea's resilience, illicit networks, and external assistance.

Regional security concerns related to North Korea's nuclear program necessitate ongoing engagement, dialogue, and diplomatic efforts. The objective remains the peaceful denuclearization of the Korean Peninsula, ensuring regional stability, and addressing the broader security concerns raised by North Korea's nuclear ambitions.

By examining the nuclear ambitions of North Korea and the regional security concerns they entail, we can gain insights into the complex power dynamics, geopolitical challenges, and the imperative for sustained diplomatic efforts. In the subsequent sections of this chapter, we will explore the role of international actors, regional responses, and potential pathways for resolving the nuclear issue.

Understanding the nuclear ambitions and regional security concerns is crucial in comprehending the broader dynamics of power, human rights, and civil liberties within North Korea and its impact on the international community.

Chapter 5: Power Projection and Geopolitical Influence

Authoritarian Regimes and Soft Power Strategies

Authoritarian regimes employ various strategies to project power and extend their geopolitical influence. This chapter explores the concept of soft power and how authoritarian regimes utilize soft power strategies to shape international narratives, influence public opinion, and advance their interests on the global stage.

Soft power, as coined by Joseph Nye, refers to a nation's ability to influence others through non-coercive means, such as culture, values, diplomacy, and international policies. While traditionally associated with democratic countries, authoritarian regimes have increasingly recognized the value of soft power in achieving their geopolitical objectives.

One way in which authoritarian regimes deploy soft power is through cultural diplomacy. They use cultural events, exhibitions, and exchanges to promote their cultural heritage and traditions, thereby enhancing their international reputation and fostering a positive image. Through cultural exports, such as films, music, and art, they seek to shape perceptions, appeal to global audiences, and create a sense of affinity or fascination with their societies.

Additionally, authoritarian regimes invest in media outlets, broadcasting networks, and news agencies to project their narratives and shape international public opinion. State-controlled media outlets allow them to control information flows, shape narratives, and influence global discourses on key issues. Through strategic dissemination of news, propaganda, and disinformation, they aim to sway international perceptions and garner support for their policies.

Economic influence is another tool employed by authoritarian regimes to exert soft power. They utilize economic partnerships, investments, and development projects to expand their influence, gain leverage, and create dependencies. By providing economic aid, loans, and infrastructure development, they can establish economic ties and secure political loyalty from recipient countries.

Furthermore, authoritarian regimes often engage in public diplomacy, utilizing diplomatic missions, cultural centers, and international organizations to extend their soft power influence. They engage in strategic alliances, coalition building, and diplomatic maneuvers to shape international norms, challenge human rights frameworks, and advocate for their preferred policies.

It is important to recognize that the soft power strategies employed by authoritarian regimes often come with hidden agendas and can be accompanied by human rights abuses or efforts to suppress dissent. While these regimes may present a positive image abroad, their domestic realities may tell a different story.

Understanding the use of soft power strategies by authoritarian regimes is essential for comprehending the power dynamics, geopolitical shifts, and the challenges they pose to democratic systems and human rights. In the subsequent sections of this chapter, we will explore the economic influence and debt diplomacy, proxy conflicts, and case studies of power projection in different regions.

By examining the soft power strategies employed by authoritarian regimes, we can gain insights into their methods of consolidating power, shaping narratives, and advancing their geopolitical interests. It also underscores the importance of promoting democratic values, safeguarding human rights, and countering the negative impacts of authoritarian soft power.

Economic Influence and Debt Diplomacy

Authoritarian regimes often employ economic influence and debt diplomacy as powerful tools for projecting power and extending their geopolitical influence. This chapter explores how these regimes utilize economic strategies to gain leverage, create dependencies, and advance their interests on the global stage.

Economic influence is a key element of the power projection employed by authoritarian regimes. These regimes leverage their economic strength to forge economic partnerships, secure trade agreements, and invest in infrastructure projects abroad. By providing financial assistance, loans, and investments, they establish economic ties and gain political loyalty from recipient countries.

One notable aspect of economic influence is debt diplomacy. Authoritarian regimes strategically extend loans and financial assistance to developing countries, often with conditions that serve their own interests. They create a debt burden for these countries, which gives the authoritarian lender significant leverage and influence over the debtor nations. In some cases, this debt burden can be used as a tool for extracting political concessions or securing control over strategic assets.

Moreover, economic influence allows authoritarian regimes to shape global economic institutions and norms. They seek to challenge the existing international economic order and advocate for alternative models that align with their own interests. By establishing new financial institutions, funding development projects, and promoting regional economic integration, these regimes aim to reshape global economic structures and reduce the influence of democratic powers.

However, the economic influence of authoritarian regimes is not without controversy. There are concerns about the transparency, sustainability, and potential negative impacts of their economic initiatives. Debt traps, where recipient countries become heavily indebted and face difficulties in repayment, raise concerns about the long-term consequences of these economic partnerships. There are also concerns about the environmental and social impacts of infrastructure projects carried out by authoritarian regimes.

Understanding the dynamics of economic influence and debt diplomacy employed by authoritarian regimes is crucial for comprehending power dynamics, geopolitical shifts, and the challenges they pose to global governance and democratic systems. In the subsequent sections of this chapter, we will explore proxy conflicts and regional power dynamics, as well as present case studies of economic influence in different regions.

By examining the economic influence and debt diplomacy strategies employed by authoritarian regimes, we can gain insights into their methods of consolidating power, shaping global economic structures, and extending their geopolitical influence. It also highlights the importance of promoting transparency, sustainability, and responsible lending practices in the international economic system.

Proxy Conflicts and Regional Power Dynamics

Authoritarian regimes often engage in proxy conflicts as a means to extend their power, exert influence, and shape regional dynamics. This chapter explores how these regimes utilize proxy conflicts and navigate regional power dynamics to advance their geopolitical interests and project influence on the global stage.

Proxy conflicts refer to conflicts in which external powers support and empower local actors, often providing them with military, financial, or political support. Authoritarian regimes frequently exploit such conflicts to extend their influence and advance their strategic objectives while minimizing direct involvement and mitigating the risk of direct confrontation with opposing powers.

These regimes employ several strategies in proxy conflicts. They provide military aid, weapons, training, and intelligence to proxy groups, enabling them to assert control over territories and challenge existing power structures. By doing so, they create a network of loyal proxies that act as a buffer and advance their interests in the region.

Regional power dynamics play a crucial role in these proxy conflicts. Authoritarian regimes seek to influence and shape the balance of power in the region, often by backing factions aligned with their own interests. By strategically leveraging their support to local actors, they can disrupt regional stability, challenge the influence of rival powers, and establish themselves as key players in regional affairs.

Proxy conflicts not only allow authoritarian regimes to extend their influence but also enable them to project power beyond their borders. These conflicts create opportunities for resource extraction, economic gain, and territorial expansion, all of which contribute to their broader geopolitical ambitions.

However, proxy conflicts also have significant humanitarian consequences. The involvement of external powers prolongs conflicts, exacerbates violence, and leads to the displacement of civilian populations. Proxy conflicts often fuel regional instability and contribute to the erosion of human rights and civil liberties.

Understanding the dynamics of proxy conflicts and regional power dynamics is crucial for comprehending the power projection strategies employed by authoritarian regimes and their impact on regional stability. In the subsequent sections of this chapter, we will explore case studies of proxy conflicts in different regions, analyze their geopolitical implications, and assess the international response to these conflicts.

By examining the proxy conflicts and regional power dynamics employed by authoritarian regimes, we can gain insights into their methods of projecting power, extending influence, and shaping the geopolitical landscape. It also underscores the importance of promoting conflict resolution, regional cooperation, and multilateral engagement to address the root causes of proxy conflicts and foster regional stability.

Case Studies of Power Projection in Different Regions

Authoritarian regimes employ various strategies to project power and extend their geopolitical influence in different regions around the world. This chapter examines case studies of power projection by authoritarian regimes in distinct geographic areas, shedding light on their tactics, regional dynamics, and global implications.

1. Case Study: China's Belt and Road Initiative (BRI) in Eurasia China's ambitious Belt and Road Initiative serves as a prime example of power projection in Eurasia. Through massive infrastructure investments, economic partnerships, and trade agreements, China aims to enhance its economic and strategic influence in Central Asia, the Middle East, and Europe. This case study explores the drivers, impacts, and challenges associated with China's BRI and its implications for regional dynamics.

2. Case Study: Russia's Influence in Eastern Europe Russia's engagement in Eastern Europe demonstrates its power projection strategies in the region. By leveraging historical ties, energy resources, and cultural connections, Russia exerts influence over neighboring countries, seeking to maintain political and economic control. This case study delves into Russia's tactics, regional power dynamics, and

the impact of its actions on the sovereignty and democratic aspirations of Eastern European nations.

3. Case Study: Saudi Arabia's Role in the Middle East Saudi Arabia's power projection in the Middle East is driven by its political, religious, and economic interests. With its vast oil wealth and leadership in the Arab world, Saudi Arabia plays a pivotal role in shaping regional dynamics. This case study examines Saudi Arabia's involvement in regional conflicts, its religious influence, and its rivalry with Iran, shedding light on the power struggles and human rights challenges in the Middle East.

4. Case Study: North Korea's Nuclear Program and Regional Security North Korea's pursuit of nuclear weapons has significant regional and global implications. By developing nuclear capabilities, North Korea seeks to enhance its security, assert its sovereignty, and gain leverage in international negotiations. This case study analyzes the regional security concerns arising from North Korea's nuclear ambitions, the impact on neighboring countries, and the international community's response.

5. Case Study: Iran's Influence in the Middle East Iran's regional power projection is characterized by its involvement in regional conflicts, support for proxy groups, and ideological influence. Iran seeks to establish itself as a

dominant player in the Middle East, challenging the traditional power balance. This case study explores Iran's strategies, its rivalry with Saudi Arabia, and the implications for regional stability and security.

Through these case studies, we gain valuable insights into the power projection tactics employed by authoritarian regimes in different regions. Examining the dynamics, challenges, and implications of their actions allows us to better understand the complex interplay of power, geopolitics, and human rights in the international arena.

Chapter 6: Human Rights and Civil Liberties
Universal Declaration of Human Rights and its Impact

The Universal Declaration of Human Rights (UDHR), adopted by the United Nations General Assembly in 1948, stands as a landmark document in the promotion and protection of human rights worldwide. This chapter delves into the origins, principles, and impact of the UDHR, examining its significance in the context of authoritarian regimes and their treatment of human rights and civil liberties.

1. Historical Context and Development of the UDHR This section provides a historical overview of the events and circumstances that led to the creation of the UDHR. It explores the aftermath of World War II, the horrors of the Holocaust, and the aspirations for a more just and humane world order. It also discusses the drafting process, the contributions of key individuals, and the international consensus that emerged around the principles of human rights.

2. Key Principles and Provisions of the UDHR This section explores the fundamental principles enshrined in the UDHR, including the right to life, liberty, and security of person; the prohibition of torture and inhumane treatment;

the right to freedom of thought, conscience, and religion; and the right to equality before the law. It examines how these principles serve as a universal standard for human rights, transcending cultural, political, and religious differences.

3. Impact of the UDHR on International Human Rights Framework The UDHR served as a catalyst for the development of an extensive body of international human rights law. This section explores how the principles of the UDHR influenced the creation of binding human rights treaties, regional human rights systems, and domestic legal frameworks. It highlights the significance of the UDHR in shaping the global human rights discourse and providing a basis for accountability and advocacy.

4. Challenges and Limitations in Implementing the UDHR Despite its significance, the implementation of the UDHR faces challenges and limitations, particularly in the context of authoritarian regimes. This section examines the ways in which authoritarian regimes often undermine or disregard the principles of the UDHR. It discusses the challenges of enforcement, the lack of accountability mechanisms, and the selective interpretation of human rights by repressive governments.

5. Role of Civil Society and Advocacy in Promoting Human Rights The UDHR has been a catalyst for civil society activism and advocacy efforts worldwide. This section explores the role of civil society organizations, human rights defenders, and grassroots movements in promoting and protecting human rights. It highlights the power of collective action and the importance of engaging with authoritarian regimes to effect positive change.

6. International Organizations and the UDHR This section examines the role of international organizations, such as the United Nations and its specialized agencies, in promoting and monitoring the implementation of the UDHR. It discusses the mechanisms for reporting, reviewing, and addressing human rights violations and the challenges of engaging with authoritarian regimes within these frameworks.

Understanding the Universal Declaration of Human Rights and its impact is essential for comprehending the significance of human rights in the context of authoritarian regimes. By recognizing the principles and values enshrined in the UDHR, we can better advocate for the protection and promotion of human rights, challenge oppressive regimes, and foster a more just and inclusive world.

Challenges to Human Rights in Authoritarian Regimes

Authoritarian regimes present significant challenges to the protection and promotion of human rights and civil liberties. This chapter delves into the complexities and specific challenges that arise in such regimes, analyzing the factors that contribute to the suppression and violation of human rights. By examining these challenges, we can gain a deeper understanding of the obstacles faced by individuals and groups striving for freedom and dignity in authoritarian contexts.

1. Concentration of Power and Lack of Accountability One of the primary challenges in authoritarian regimes is the concentration of power in the hands of a single individual or a small group. This concentration often leads to the erosion of checks and balances, weakening accountability mechanisms and enabling human rights abuses. This section explores the mechanisms used by authoritarian leaders to consolidate power and evade accountability, such as through control over the judiciary, security forces, and media.

2. Suppression of Freedom of Expression and Information Authoritarian regimes frequently suppress freedom of expression and control the flow of information to maintain their grip on power. This section examines the

tactics used to stifle dissent, including censorship, internet restrictions, and harassment of journalists, activists, and human rights defenders. It also explores the consequences of restricted access to information, including the manipulation of public opinion and the perpetuation of disinformation.

3. Arbitrary Detention, Torture, and Abuse of Power Another significant challenge in authoritarian regimes is the prevalence of arbitrary detention, torture, and abuse of power by state authorities. This section explores the use of surveillance, secret police, and extrajudicial measures to suppress opposition, silence dissent, and instill fear in the population. It also examines the impact of these practices on the physical and psychological well-being of individuals, as well as the long-lasting societal repercussions.

4. Discrimination and Marginalization Authoritarian regimes often discriminate against certain groups based on factors such as ethnicity, religion, political beliefs, or social status. This section delves into the systemic discrimination and marginalization faced by minority communities, political dissidents, women, LGBTQ+ individuals, and other vulnerable groups. It explores the denial of equal rights, access to services, and opportunities for these marginalized populations.

5. Lack of Independent Civil Society and Human Rights Defenders Authoritarian regimes frequently undermine independent civil society organizations and human rights defenders, as they are seen as threats to their power. This section examines the challenges faced by civil society in operating freely and advocating for human rights. It explores the harassment, intimidation, and legal restrictions imposed on activists and organizations, and the impact of these actions on the defense and promotion of human rights.

6. International Response and Accountability Addressing human rights challenges in authoritarian regimes requires international engagement and accountability mechanisms. This section explores the role of international organizations, such as the United Nations, regional bodies, and human rights NGOs, in monitoring and advocating for human rights. It also discusses the limitations and obstacles in holding authoritarian regimes accountable, including issues of sovereignty, geopolitical considerations, and diplomatic challenges.

Understanding the challenges faced by individuals and communities in authoritarian regimes is crucial for developing effective strategies to promote human rights and protect civil liberties. By recognizing these challenges, we can work towards building alliances, strengthening international cooperation, and supporting local efforts to foster change and advance human rights in authoritarian contexts.

Activism and Advocacy for Human Rights

Activism and advocacy play a crucial role in promoting and defending human rights and civil liberties, especially in the face of authoritarian regimes. This chapter explores the power of activism, the challenges activists face, and the strategies they employ to effect change and create a more just and inclusive society.

1. The Role of Human Rights Activism This section introduces the significance of human rights activism in authoritarian contexts. It highlights the importance of individuals and groups dedicated to upholding and protecting human rights, and how their work contributes to raising awareness, challenging oppressive systems, and demanding accountability from authoritarian regimes.

2. Strategies and Approaches in Human Rights Advocacy Effective human rights advocacy requires careful planning and the implementation of strategic approaches. This section examines various strategies employed by activists, including legal advocacy, grassroots mobilization, public campaigns, digital activism, and engaging with international human rights mechanisms. It explores how these approaches can amplify voices, expose human rights abuses, and put pressure on authoritarian regimes to respect and protect human rights.

3. Challenges and Risks Faced by Human Rights Activists Engaging in human rights activism in authoritarian regimes is not without risks. This section delves into the challenges faced by activists, such as surveillance, harassment, intimidation, arbitrary detention, and physical violence. It highlights the personal sacrifices made by activists who face these risks in their pursuit of justice and human rights.

4. Digital Activism and Online Spaces The digital age has provided new avenues for human rights activism and advocacy. This section explores the role of digital platforms, social media, and online spaces in amplifying human rights messages, organizing campaigns, and circumventing censorship. It also discusses the challenges and risks associated with digital activism, such as online surveillance and state-controlled internet infrastructure.

5. International Solidarity and Collaboration Human rights activism often transcends national borders, relying on international solidarity and collaboration. This section examines the importance of building alliances with international organizations, human rights NGOs, and like-minded individuals and groups across the globe. It explores how international support can bolster the work of activists,

provide protection, and exert pressure on authoritarian regimes.

6. Impact and Success Stories Despite the challenges, human rights activism has achieved significant victories in authoritarian contexts. This section showcases success stories of activists and advocacy campaigns that have led to positive change, improved human rights conditions, and challenged authoritarian regimes. It highlights the transformative power of grassroots movements, the importance of perseverance, and the long-term impact of sustained activism.

By examining the role of activism and advocacy for human rights, we gain a deeper understanding of the resilience and determination of individuals and communities striving for justice and freedom in authoritarian regimes. Their stories inspire us to stand in solidarity, support their efforts, and work towards a world where human rights and civil liberties are respected and protected for all.

Role of International Organizations in Promoting Human Rights

International organizations play a crucial role in promoting and protecting human rights around the world. This chapter explores the significance of international organizations in advocating for human rights, monitoring human rights abuses, and providing support to individuals and communities affected by authoritarian regimes.

1. Introduction to International Organizations and Human Rights This section provides an overview of international organizations dedicated to promoting human rights, such as the United Nations (UN), Amnesty International, Human Rights Watch, and regional bodies like the European Court of Human Rights and the Inter-American Commission on Human Rights. It highlights the importance of their work in addressing human rights violations and creating global standards for human rights protection.

2. The United Nations and Human Rights The United Nations is at the forefront of the international human rights regime. This section examines the UN's role in promoting human rights through the Universal Declaration of Human Rights, treaty bodies, special rapporteurs, and the Human Rights Council. It explores how the UN investigates human

rights abuses, advocates for justice, and engages with authoritarian regimes to hold them accountable for their actions.

3. Regional Human Rights Bodies Regional organizations also play a vital role in promoting human rights within specific geographic areas. This section focuses on regional bodies like the European Court of Human Rights, the African Commission on Human and Peoples' Rights, and the Inter-American Commission on Human Rights. It discusses their mandates, mechanisms for addressing human rights violations, and their impact on regional human rights protection.

4. Human Rights Monitoring and Reporting International organizations engage in human rights monitoring and reporting to document human rights abuses and provide accurate information to the global community. This section explores the methodologies employed by these organizations, including fact-finding missions, on-the-ground investigations, and testimonies from victims and witnesses. It also examines the challenges they face in gathering evidence and ensuring the credibility of their reports.

5. Advocacy and Diplomacy International organizations engage in advocacy and diplomacy to influence

authoritarian regimes and promote human rights. This section explores their strategies, such as public statements, diplomatic pressure, and engagement with governments and civil society organizations. It also discusses the challenges and limitations they encounter in navigating diplomatic relations and balancing political considerations.

6. Support and Assistance for Affected Individuals and Communities International organizations provide support and assistance to individuals and communities affected by authoritarian regimes. This section examines their efforts in areas such as legal aid, capacity-building, psychosocial support, and humanitarian assistance. It highlights the importance of empowering affected populations and enabling them to seek justice and redress for human rights violations.

7. Collaboration with Civil Society and Grassroots Movements International organizations collaborate with civil society organizations and grassroots movements to amplify their impact and promote human rights at the local level. This section explores partnerships and cooperation between international organizations and local actors, emphasizing the importance of including diverse perspectives and voices in human rights advocacy.

8. Assessing the Effectiveness of International Organizations The effectiveness of international organizations in promoting human rights in authoritarian regimes is a complex issue. This section examines the challenges and limitations faced by these organizations, including political constraints, resource limitations, and the complexities of engaging with authoritarian regimes. It also evaluates their successes and areas for improvement, offering recommendations for enhancing their effectiveness.

By examining the role of international organizations in promoting human rights, we gain a deeper understanding of the global efforts to protect human rights, hold authoritarian regimes accountable, and support affected individuals and communities. Their work contributes to building a world where human rights and civil liberties are universally respected and protected.

Chapter 7: Democratization and Transitioning from Authoritarianism

Factors Affecting Democratization Processes

Democratization is a complex and multifaceted process influenced by various factors. This chapter explores the key elements that shape the transition from authoritarianism to democracy, analyzing both internal and external dynamics that impact the democratization processes.

1. Introduction to Democratization This section provides an overview of the concept of democratization, emphasizing its significance as a transformative process that involves the establishment of democratic institutions, respect for human rights, and the participation of citizens in decision-making. It highlights the challenges and opportunities associated with democratization.

2. Historical and Cultural Context The historical and cultural context of a country plays a crucial role in shaping democratization processes. This section examines how factors such as colonial legacies, cultural norms, and historical experiences impact the path towards democracy. It explores the influence of historical events, social movements, and cultural values on the willingness and readiness of a society to embrace democratic principles.

3. Political Leadership and Elite Behavior The role of political leaders and elites is instrumental in driving or hindering democratization efforts. This section explores the impact of political leadership on democratic transitions, examining the strategies and motivations of leaders, their commitment to democratic principles, and their ability to build consensus and manage conflicts. It also discusses the influence of political parties, interest groups, and other influential actors in shaping the democratization process.

4. Socioeconomic Factors Socioeconomic conditions can either facilitate or impede democratization. This section analyzes the relationship between socioeconomic factors and democratization, such as income inequality, poverty, access to education, and economic development. It explores how economic stability, social mobility, and the distribution of resources influence the prospects for democratization.

5. Civil Society and Social Movements The strength and resilience of civil society and social movements are vital for successful democratization. This section examines the role of civil society organizations, grassroots movements, and advocacy groups in mobilizing citizens, promoting democratic values, and advocating for political reforms. It discusses how civil society engagement and collective action can shape the democratization process.

6. External Factors and International Support
External factors, including international actors and support, can significantly influence democratization processes. This section explores the role of external actors such as regional organizations, international institutions, and foreign governments in facilitating or obstructing democratization. It discusses the impact of foreign aid, diplomatic pressure, and conditional assistance on democratic transitions.

7. Institutional Design and Constitutional Framework
The design of democratic institutions and the constitution is critical for the consolidation of democracy. This section examines the importance of creating inclusive and accountable institutions, ensuring the separation of powers, establishing an independent judiciary, and protecting fundamental rights and freedoms. It explores the challenges and opportunities in designing effective democratic institutions.

8. Transitional Justice and Reconciliation Addressing past human rights abuses and promoting reconciliation are integral to successful democratization processes. This section discusses the significance of transitional justice mechanisms, including truth commissions, prosecutions, reparations, and reconciliation initiatives. It explores how dealing with the

legacies of authoritarian rule contributes to long-term stability and democratic consolidation.

9. Challenges and Pitfalls in Democratization Democratization processes are often faced with numerous challenges and potential pitfalls. This section examines common challenges, such as political polarization, ethnic or religious tensions, corruption, and the risk of democratic backsliding. It discusses the importance of navigating these challenges and implementing effective strategies to safeguard and strengthen democratic gains.

By exploring and analyzing these factors, this chapter provides a comprehensive understanding of the complexities and dynamics involved in the transition from authoritarianism to democracy. It highlights the importance of considering various elements and adopting context-specific approaches to promote successful democratization processes.

Historical Examples of Successful Transitions

Democratization is a complex and challenging process, but history has shown us that successful transitions from authoritarianism to democracy are possible. This chapter explores several historical examples of successful democratization, highlighting the key factors and strategies that contributed to their success.

1. Introduction to Successful Transitions This section provides an overview of the importance of studying historical cases of successful democratization. It emphasizes the potential lessons and insights that can be drawn from these cases and how they can inform and guide current and future democratization efforts.

2. Spain's Transition to Democracy The transition from General Francisco Franco's authoritarian regime to democracy in Spain serves as a significant historical example of successful democratization. This section examines the factors that led to Spain's successful transition, including political reforms, the role of key political actors, and the establishment of democratic institutions.

3. South Africa's Transition from Apartheid South Africa's transition from apartheid to democracy under the leadership of Nelson Mandela is another inspiring case of successful democratization. This section explores the

challenges faced during this transition, such as reconciling a deeply divided society and establishing a new political framework based on inclusivity and equality.

4. Eastern Europe's Transition after the Fall of the Soviet Union The collapse of the Soviet Union and the subsequent transition of Eastern European countries provide valuable insights into successful democratization. This section examines the experiences of countries like Poland, Hungary, and the Czech Republic, highlighting the role of civil society movements, political leadership, and the adoption of democratic institutions.

5. Chile's Return to Democracy Chile's transition from the military dictatorship of Augusto Pinochet to democracy is a notable case in Latin America. This section analyzes the factors that facilitated Chile's successful transition, including the use of referendums, truth and reconciliation commissions, and the gradual restoration of democratic institutions.

6. The African Renaissance: Botswana and Ghana Botswana and Ghana are examples of successful democratization efforts in Africa. This section explores the factors that contributed to their success, including strong leadership, commitment to the rule of law, and inclusive

political processes. It also discusses the challenges they faced and how they overcame them.

7. Lessons and Commonalities Drawing from these historical examples, this section identifies commonalities and lessons that can be applied to future democratization processes. It highlights the importance of inclusive political dialogue, effective leadership, the rule of law, civil society engagement, and international support.

8. Contemporary Challenges and Future Directions This section discusses the contemporary challenges that democratization faces in the 21st century, such as rising populism, democratic backsliding, and external interference. It also explores future directions for successful democratization, including the importance of digital technologies, youth engagement, and addressing social and economic inequalities.

By examining these historical examples of successful democratization, we can gain valuable insights into the complexities and strategies that contribute to a successful transition from authoritarianism to democracy. These cases demonstrate that with the right conditions, leadership, and societal engagement, democratic transformation is possible.

Challenges and Pitfalls in Transitioning to Democracy

Transitioning from authoritarianism to democracy is a complex and delicate process that entails numerous challenges and pitfalls. This chapter examines the key obstacles that arise during democratization efforts, providing insights into the difficulties faced by societies undergoing such transitions.

1. Introduction to Challenges and Pitfalls This section introduces the concept of challenges and pitfalls in democratization, emphasizing their significance in understanding the intricacies of transitioning from authoritarianism to democracy. It highlights the need for careful analysis and proactive measures to overcome these obstacles.

2. Weak Institutions and Rule of Law One of the primary challenges in democratization is the weakness of institutions and the rule of law. This section explores how authoritarian regimes often undermine institutions and establish a culture of impunity. It also examines the consequences of weak institutions, including corruption, lack of accountability, and a diminished trust in democratic processes.

3. Polarization and Divisive Politics Transitioning to democracy often faces the challenge of polarization and divisive politics. This section delves into the causes and consequences of political polarization, including ethnic, religious, or ideological divisions. It examines how these divisions can hinder the development of inclusive democratic systems and contribute to social tensions and conflicts.

4. Economic Inequalities and Social Discontent The persistence of economic inequalities and social discontent can undermine democratization efforts. This section analyzes how socioeconomic disparities, poverty, and lack of opportunities can fuel social unrest and disillusionment. It also explores the importance of addressing these inequalities as part of a comprehensive democratization process.

5. Transitional Justice and Dealing with the Past Transitional justice, including the prosecution of human rights abuses and addressing past injustices, is a critical challenge during democratization. This section examines the complexities of transitional justice processes, including the need for truth and reconciliation mechanisms, reparations, and the delicate balance between accountability and national reconciliation.

6. External Interference and Influence External interference and influence pose significant challenges to

democratization processes. This section explores how external actors, such as neighboring countries, global powers, or non-state actors, can undermine democratic transitions through various means, including support for authoritarian regimes or manipulation of political processes.

7. Democratic Backsliding and Authoritarian Resurgence One of the greatest pitfalls in democratization is the potential for democratic backsliding and the resurgence of authoritarianism. This section examines how democratic institutions and values can be undermined, eroded, or subverted over time. It highlights the importance of safeguarding democratic gains and remaining vigilant against authoritarian threats.

8. Strategies for Overcoming Challenges This section discusses strategies and approaches to overcome the challenges and pitfalls in transitioning to democracy. It explores the significance of inclusive political dialogue, fostering civic engagement, building strong democratic institutions, promoting transparency and accountability, and ensuring the protection of human rights and civil liberties.

9. Lessons Learned and Future Directions Drawing from the analysis of challenges and pitfalls, this section identifies key lessons learned and suggests future directions for successful democratization efforts. It emphasizes the

need for long-term commitment, adaptive strategies, international cooperation, and the engagement of civil society in shaping democratic processes.

By understanding and addressing the challenges and pitfalls in transitioning to democracy, societies can develop effective strategies and mechanisms to navigate the complexities of democratization. This chapter aims to provide valuable insights into these obstacles and to inform efforts to build resilient and inclusive democratic systems.

Role of Civil Society and External Actors in Democratization

The democratization process and transition from authoritarianism rely on the active involvement of various actors, including civil society organizations and external actors. This chapter explores the crucial roles these entities play in promoting and sustaining democratization efforts.

1. Introduction to Civil Society and External Actors This section provides an overview of civil society organizations and external actors, emphasizing their significance in democratization processes. It explores their unique roles, motivations, and the dynamics of their engagement in fostering democratic change.

2. Civil Society and Democratic Advocacy Civil society organizations play a pivotal role in democratization by advocating for democratic values, promoting human rights, and mobilizing citizens. This section delves into the importance of an active civil society in challenging authoritarianism, fostering civic engagement, and contributing to the development of democratic institutions.

3. Civil Society and Social Movements Social movements often emerge as catalysts for democratization. This section examines the role of civil society organizations in facilitating and supporting social movements, exploring

how they can channel public grievances, mobilize collective action, and drive social and political change.

4. Civil Society and Monitoring Elections Monitoring elections is crucial for ensuring free and fair democratic processes. This section discusses the role of civil society organizations in election monitoring, including voter education, observing electoral processes, and advocating for transparency and accountability in elections.

5. Civil Society and Human Rights Protection Protecting human rights is an integral part of democratization. This section explores how civil society organizations contribute to human rights protection through documentation, advocacy, legal aid, and the promotion of a culture of human rights within society.

6. Civil Society and Accountability Mechanisms Accountability mechanisms are essential for consolidating democracy. This section examines the role of civil society organizations in holding governments accountable, monitoring the actions of public officials, and advocating for transparency and integrity in governance.

7. External Actors and Democracy Promotion External actors, such as international organizations, regional bodies, and donor countries, have a significant influence on democratization processes. This section explores the role of

external actors in supporting democratic transitions, providing financial assistance, technical expertise, and promoting democratic norms and values.

8. External Actors and Diplomatic Pressure Diplomatic pressure can be a potent tool in encouraging democratic reforms. This section examines how external actors can exert diplomatic pressure on authoritarian regimes, imposing sanctions, leveraging trade agreements, or using international platforms to advocate for democratic change.

9. External Actors and Capacity Building Capacity building is crucial for successful democratization. This section explores the role of external actors in supporting capacity-building efforts, including providing technical assistance, training programs, and knowledge transfer to strengthen democratic institutions and processes.

10. External Actors and Democratization Challenges External actors face challenges and dilemmas in their engagement in democratization processes. This section examines the complexities and potential pitfalls of external involvement, including accusations of interference, balancing national interests, and the importance of respecting local contexts and ownership.

11. Synergy and Collaboration between Civil Society and External Actors This section emphasizes the importance of synergy and collaboration between civil society organizations and external actors. It explores how effective partnerships can leverage resources, expertise, and networks to enhance democratization efforts and foster sustainable democratic transitions.

12. Lessons Learned and Best Practices Drawing from the analysis of the roles of civil society and external actors, this section identifies key lessons learned and best practices in democratization. It highlights successful cases, challenges encountered, and provides recommendations for future democratization efforts.

Conclusion The chapter concludes by underscoring the critical roles of civil society organizations and external actors in supporting democratization and transitioning from authoritarianism. It emphasizes the need for continued collaboration, adaptive strategies, and the promotion of democratic values to build inclusive, accountable, and resilient democratic societies.

Conclusion

Recap of Key Insights on Authoritarian Regimes

Throughout this book, we have delved into the dynamics of authoritarian regimes, their consolidation of power, suppression of dissent, and their impact on human rights and civil liberties. In this final section, we will recapitulate the key insights and findings discussed in the previous chapters.

1. Authoritarianism: Understanding the Phenomenon

- Authoritarianism is a complex political system characterized by centralized power, limited political competition, and restricted civil liberties.

- Various factors contribute to the rise and endurance of authoritarian regimes, including historical context, socio-economic conditions, and geopolitical dynamics.

2. China: Evolution of an Authoritarian Regime

- China's authoritarian regime has undergone significant transformation since the establishment of the People's Republic in 1949.

- The Communist Party's control over political, economic, and social spheres has played a central role in maintaining its power.

- China's economic reforms have contributed to its political stability, but have also led to increased inequality and concerns about human rights.

3. Russia: Consolidation of Power under Vladimir Putin

- Post-Soviet Russia has witnessed the consolidation of power under Vladimir Putin, who has centralized authority, weakened political opposition, and exerted control over the media.

- The Kremlin's influence over key sectors of society, including the economy and the judiciary, has limited democratic processes and undermined civil liberties.

- Russia's actions in the international arena have further shaped its domestic politics and impacted human rights within and beyond its borders.

4. Saudi Arabia: Monarchy, Religion, and Human Rights

- Saudi Arabia's political system revolves around the monarchy and its close alignment with religious institutions.

- The role of religion, particularly the application of Sharia law, has influenced the country's governance and posed challenges to human rights, particularly women's rights and freedom of expression.

- Saudi Arabia's influence in the Middle East has significant implications for regional dynamics, including conflicts and geopolitical alignments.

5. North Korea: Kim Dynasty and Totalitarian Rule

- North Korea's authoritarian regime, led by the Kim dynasty, maintains tight control over all aspects of society through state propaganda, surveillance, and isolationism.

- The regime's human rights abuses, including political repression, censorship, and forced labor, have drawn international condemnation.

- North Korea's nuclear ambitions have heightened regional security concerns, leading to tensions and diplomatic challenges.

6. Power Projection and Geopolitical Influence

- Authoritarian regimes utilize various strategies to project power and exert influence on the global stage.

- Economic influence, including debt diplomacy, has become a prominent tool in securing political alliances and advancing national interests.

- Proxy conflicts and regional power dynamics serve as arenas for authoritarian regimes to extend their influence and shape geopolitical landscapes.

7. Human Rights and Civil Liberties in Authoritarian Regimes

- The Universal Declaration of Human Rights provides a universal framework for promoting and protecting human rights, but its implementation faces significant challenges in authoritarian contexts.

- Activism and advocacy for human rights play a crucial role in challenging oppressive regimes, raising awareness, and promoting change.

- International organizations, such as the United Nations and regional bodies, have a responsibility to monitor human rights violations and support initiatives that promote human rights in authoritarian regimes.

8. Democratization and Transitioning from Authoritarianism

- Successful transitions from authoritarianism to democracy depend on a range of factors, including societal conditions, political will, and external support.

- Historical examples of successful transitions offer valuable insights into the challenges faced and the strategies employed.

- However, transitioning to democracy is fraught with challenges and pitfalls, including political instability, social divisions, and the risk of relapse into authoritarianism.

In conclusion, this book has provided a comprehensive examination of authoritarian regimes, their power dynamics, and their impact on human rights and civil liberties. It has underscored the significance of understanding these regimes' historical contexts, consolidation of power, and the challenges they pose to democratic values. By shedding light on these issues, we hope to foster a deeper understanding of authoritarianism and stimulate discussions on promoting human rights and democratic principles in our global society.

Balancing Power, Stability, and Human Right

Throughout this book, we have examined the intricate dynamics of authoritarian regimes and their impact on human rights and civil liberties. In this final section, we will delve into the complex challenge of balancing power, stability, and human rights in the context of authoritarian governance.

1. The Authoritarian Dilemma: Authoritarian regimes face a fundamental dilemma when it comes to power and stability. On one hand, they strive to maintain a firm grip on power to safeguard their interests and the stability of the regime. On the other hand, they must navigate the demands and expectations of their population, regional and international pressures, and the imperative to respect human rights.

2. Power Consolidation and Stability: Authoritarian regimes often concentrate power in the hands of a select few or a single individual, enabling them to make decisions swiftly and maintain control. This consolidation of power is seen as essential for stability, as it minimizes dissent, prevents political upheavals, and ensures continuity of governance. However, such concentration of power can lead to abuses and violations of human rights.

3. Human Rights Challenges: The pursuit of power and stability in authoritarian regimes can come at the expense of human rights. Political opponents, dissidents, and activists advocating for change often face repression, censorship, and imprisonment. Civil liberties, such as freedom of speech, assembly, and association, are curtailed to maintain the regime's control. Discrimination, inequality, and persecution become prevalent, eroding the principles of justice and fairness.

4. Justifications for Power Concentration: Authoritarian regimes often justify their power concentration by highlighting the need for stability, economic development, and national security. They argue that robust control is necessary to protect citizens from internal and external threats, foster economic growth, and maintain social order. However, these justifications can serve as a veil for suppressing dissent and violating human rights.

5. International Relations and Realpolitik: The international community plays a crucial role in balancing power, stability, and human rights in authoritarian regimes. Global powers, regional organizations, and civil society groups face the challenge of engaging with these regimes while holding them accountable for human rights abuses.

Striking a delicate balance between engagement and condemnation is essential to promote positive change and protect human rights.

6. Rethinking Approaches: Finding a balance between power, stability, and human rights requires rethinking traditional approaches to governance and international relations. It entails promoting democratic values, advocating for human rights, and supporting civil society organizations within authoritarian contexts. Economic incentives can be leveraged to encourage reforms, ensuring that development goes hand in hand with human rights protections.

7. Engagement and Dialogue: Constructive engagement and dialogue can be powerful tools in promoting human rights and fostering gradual change within authoritarian regimes. Encouraging open discussions, promoting the rule of law, and supporting independent media outlets can contribute to a more inclusive and accountable governance system. Engaging with a broad spectrum of actors, including the regime, opposition groups, and civil society, can help build trust and facilitate positive transformations.

8. Long-Term Strategies: Efforts to balance power, stability, and human rights should encompass long-term strategies that focus on education, capacity-building, and

institutional reforms. Empowering the population through education and civic participation can lay the groundwork for a more inclusive and democratic society. Strengthening institutions, promoting transparency, and establishing mechanisms for accountability can mitigate abuses of power and protect human rights.

In conclusion, the delicate balance between power, stability, and human rights in authoritarian regimes is a complex and multifaceted challenge. Striving for this balance requires reevaluating traditional approaches, fostering constructive engagement, and pursuing long-term strategies that empower the population and promote democratic values. By actively working towards this equilibrium, we can hope to create a future where power is balanced, stability is maintained, and human rights are respected.

The Role of International Cooperation in Addressing Authoritarianism

In this final section, we will examine the critical role of international cooperation in addressing authoritarianism and promoting human rights. Authoritarian regimes pose significant challenges to global peace, security, and the protection of human rights. Therefore, international collaboration is crucial in combating these challenges and fostering a more just and democratic world.

1. Understanding Authoritarianism's Transnational Impact: Authoritarian regimes are not confined to their national borders. They often exert influence beyond their territories, impacting neighboring countries and even global affairs. Therefore, addressing authoritarianism requires a comprehensive and coordinated international response that recognizes the transnational nature of these regimes.

2. Building International Consensus: One of the first steps in combating authoritarianism is building a consensus among the international community. By recognizing the shared values of democracy, human rights, and the rule of law, nations can work together to develop strategies and policies aimed at promoting and protecting these principles.

3. Multilateral Institutions and Mechanisms: Multilateral institutions, such as the United Nations, play a

central role in addressing authoritarianism. These institutions provide platforms for diplomatic negotiations, dialogue, and the formulation of international norms and standards. Strengthening these institutions and their mechanisms for accountability is crucial for holding authoritarian regimes accountable for their actions.

4. Economic Leverage and Sanctions: Economic cooperation and leverage can be potent tools in addressing authoritarianism. International actors can use economic incentives and sanctions to influence the behavior of authoritarian regimes. Targeted sanctions, for example, can be imposed on individuals and entities involved in human rights abuses, sending a strong message and pressuring regimes to change their practices.

5. Human Rights Advocacy: International cooperation plays a critical role in advocating for human rights and raising awareness of human rights abuses in authoritarian regimes. By supporting human rights defenders, civil society organizations, and independent media, the international community can amplify their voices and contribute to positive change on the ground.

6. Diplomacy and Engagement: Engaging authoritarian regimes diplomatically can be a challenging but necessary approach to address human rights concerns.

Diplomatic channels provide opportunities for dialogue, negotiation, and the promotion of human rights norms. While engagement must be approached cautiously, it can serve as a means to influence regimes positively and encourage reforms.

7. Supporting Civil Society and Grassroots Movements: International cooperation should focus on supporting civil society organizations and grassroots movements within authoritarian regimes. These actors play a crucial role in advocating for human rights, fostering democratic values, and promoting social and political change from within. By providing resources, training, and protection, the international community can empower these groups to make a significant impact.

8. Balancing Interests and Values: International cooperation requires a delicate balance between strategic interests and the promotion of democratic values. While nations may have diverse economic, security, and geopolitical interests, it is essential not to compromise on fundamental human rights principles. Striking a balance that respects both interests and values is a complex but necessary endeavor.

9. Long-Term Engagement and Support: Addressing authoritarianism is a long-term commitment that requires

sustained engagement and support. Efforts to promote democracy, human rights, and the rule of law must be consistent and adaptable to evolving circumstances. Investing in education, capacity-building, and institution-building can lay the foundation for lasting change.

10. Collaboration across Sectors: Addressing authoritarianism requires collaboration not only among governments but also across sectors. Cooperation between governments, civil society, academia, businesses, and the media can yield comprehensive strategies that tackle the multifaceted challenges posed by authoritarian regimes. Harnessing the collective expertise and resources of different stakeholders is crucial for success.

Conclusion:

In conclusion, international cooperation plays a vital role in addressing authoritarianism and promoting human rights globally. By building consensus, leveraging economic tools, advocating for human rights, engaging diplomatically, and supporting civil society, the international community can work together to challenge authoritarian regimes and foster a more democratic and just world. This collaborative effort requires a long-term commitment, balancing strategic interests with the promotion of universal values. By recognizing the transnational impact of authoritarianism and acting collectively, we can create a brighter future where human rights are upheld and authoritarianism is gradually diminished.

THE END

Key Terms and Definitions

To help you better understand the language and concepts related to aging and older adults, below you will find a list of key terms and their definitions.

1. Authoritarianism: A form of government characterized by the concentration of power in the hands of a single leader or a small group of individuals, often with limited or no accountability to the public. Authoritarian regimes typically suppress political opposition, restrict civil liberties, and exercise strict control over society.

2. Power: The ability to influence or control others and shape the course of events. In the context of authoritarian regimes, power refers to the concentration of political authority and decision-making in the hands of a few individuals or institutions.

3. Human Rights: Fundamental rights and freedoms to which all individuals are inherently entitled, regardless of their nationality, ethnicity, religion, gender, or any other status. Human rights include civil, political, economic, social, and cultural rights, such as the right to life, liberty, equality, and freedom of expression.

4. Civil Liberties: Basic rights and freedoms that are guaranteed and protected by the law, enabling individuals to exercise their autonomy and participate fully in society. Civil

liberties include freedom of speech, assembly, religion, and the right to a fair trial.

5. Transnational Impact: The influence or effects that extend beyond national borders. In the context of authoritarian regimes, transnational impact refers to the reach and consequences of their policies, actions, and ideologies on neighboring countries, regional stability, and global affairs.

6. International Cooperation: Collaborative efforts between nations and international organizations to address common challenges, promote shared values, and achieve collective goals. In the context of authoritarian regimes, international cooperation involves joint actions and strategies to combat authoritarianism, protect human rights, and promote democratic values.

7. Diplomacy: The practice of conducting negotiations, dialogue, and communication between nations to manage conflicts, foster understanding, and pursue common objectives. Diplomatic efforts can play a crucial role in addressing authoritarianism by engaging with authoritarian regimes, promoting human rights, and advocating for democratic reforms.

8. Multilateral Institutions: Organizations composed of multiple nations that work together to address global

issues and promote cooperation. Examples of multilateral institutions include the United Nations (UN), the World Bank, and regional organizations such as the European Union (EU) and the African Union (AU).

9. Sanctions: Measures imposed by governments or international bodies to exert pressure on authoritarian regimes and encourage policy change. Sanctions can involve economic restrictions, travel bans, asset freezes, or other penalties aimed at compelling authoritarian regimes to respect human rights and democratic principles.

10. Civil Society: The collective organizations, institutions, and individuals outside the government and business sectors that contribute to social and political life. Civil society plays a crucial role in promoting human rights, advocating for democratic values, and holding authoritarian regimes accountable.

Supporting Materials

Introduction

No specific references provided in the outline.

Chapter 1: China

Shirk, S. (2017). The Political Logic of China's Authoritarian Regime: Theories, Methods, and Measures of Its Success. Cambridge University Press. (Page numbers for specific references not provided in the outline.)

Chapter 2: Russia

Hale, H. E. (2014). Patronal Politics: Eurasian Regime Dynamics in Comparative Perspective. Cambridge University Press. (Page numbers for specific references not provided in the outline.)

Chapter 3: Saudi Arabia

Al-Rasheed, M. (2018). Muted Modernists: The Struggle over Divine Politics in Saudi Arabia. Oxford University Press. (Page numbers for specific references not provided in the outline.)

Chapter 4: North Korea

Myers, B. R. (2015). North Korea's Juche Myth. Busan University of Foreign Studies Press. (Page numbers for specific references not provided in the outline.)

Chapter 5: Power Projection and Geopolitical Influence

Nye, J. S. (2011). The Future of Power. PublicAffairs. (Page numbers for specific references not provided in the outline.)
Chapter 6: Human Rights and Civil Liberties
Ignatieff, M. (2001). Human Rights as Politics and Idolatry. Princeton University Press. (Page numbers for specific references not provided in the outline.)
Chapter 7: Democratization and Transitioning from Authoritarianism
Levitsky, S., & Way, L. A. (2010). Competitive Authoritarianism: Hybrid Regimes after the Cold War. Cambridge University Press. (Page numbers for specific references not provided in the outline.)
Conclusion
No specific references provided in the outline.